MARSHALLTOWN
YOUNG PEOPLE

This book belongs to this Marshalltown Young Person

NAME: _____

DATE: _____

Marshall T. Trowel and Family
DRYWALL

YOU CAN BE ANYTHING YOU WANT TO BE.

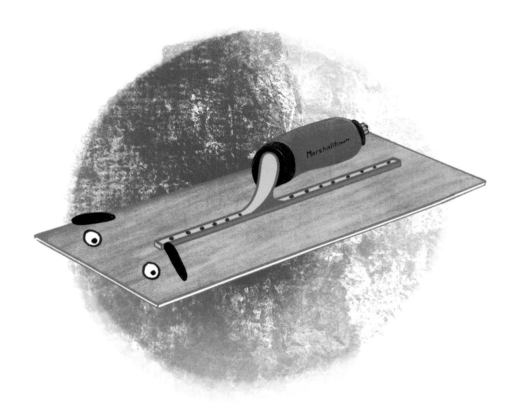

MARSHALLTOWN
® U.S.A.

A Marshalltown Book for Young People who Love Construction

Written by Joe Carter   Illustrated by Hanna Carter

Other Marshall T. Trowel and Family books:

Marshall T. Trowel and Family - Concrete - Work Hard. Work Together.

Learn more at www.marshallttrowel.com

Marshalltown Company, 104 South 8th Avenue, Marshalltown, Iowa 50158
641-753-5999 | 800-888-0127 | www.marshalltown.com

Printed in the United States of America
By Walsworth

ISBN: 978-0-578-56828-7

WITH THE PUBLICATION OF THE SECOND MARSHALL T. TROWEL AND FAMILY BOOK,

my goals are the same: to show young people the benefits of the construction trades as a great career, send a positive message, and create a story that families can enjoy together.

I have been so blessed within the community of Marshalltown, Iowa, to have so many people and businesses help support the first book. The Marshalltown Times Republican, Radio Station KFJB, and KCWI-TV in Des Moines were gems to help us spread the word. All the businesses that sold books for us in the local area were so generous to help a new author—Hellberg's Jewelers, 19 Salon and Spa, Thompson True Value, Stepping Stones Christian Bookstore, Read a Book Nook, Spahn and Rose, Home Rental Center, and Strands. I also want to thank Ozinga in Chicago for letting us take some great promotional photos around their iconic red and white striped concrete trucks.

I started writing the first Marshall T. Trowel and Family book in 2002 when my three children were 6, 8 and 12. My wife Janelle and I read books to them every night. It was a time all of us treasured. I wanted to create those same types of treasured moments with a book that would combine my world of the construction industry with cute characters who could bring the tools to life.

Janelle and I are so proud of all three of our children. Each one has embarked upon a career that seems fitting for each of them based upon the interests they had as young children. I'm confident that they realized as young people that they could be anything they wanted to be—the message of this book.

I dedicate this book to the best wife I could ever imagine, our children, and to the rest of my wonderful family who have encouraged me throughout my life. I also have to specifically call out my brother who took the time to come to my first book signing and then feverishly promoted the book to all his friends and former high school classmates! I am blessed to have my family close in my heart.

I hope that you will also hold close in your heart the young person who is reading this book with you. Maybe this young person will fall in love with construction and embark on a career that helps build a world filled with wonderful things. But no matter what, I hope this young person knows they can be anything they want to be.

I believe that the illustrations bring a children's book to life, and I don't believe anyone could have done a better job of bringing this book to life than my daughter, Hanna. While I hope the words are interesting, I've seen firsthand how young people light up when they see the characters from the first book. I don't know how a father could be more proud.

- Joe Carter

Ms. Finn was hired to hang and finish the drywall of a new home in Marshalltown, Iowa. She had been unusually busy the past year, but Ms. Finn was excited to get started on a beautiful, new home being built for Mr. Mason.

Ms. Finn had her own drywall contracting business called Marshalltown Drywall, but years earlier she had worked as part of Mr. Mason's concrete crew. She enjoyed working with her hands and quickly became one of Mr. Mason's best employees. He was proud of her and wanted Ms. Finn to keep learning and growing.

Over the years Marshalltown Drywall had become the best drywall contracting company in the state. Ms. Finn ran an impeccable business!

When Mr. Mason decided to build a new home for his family, he knew immediately that Ms. Finn would be his drywall contractor.

Ms. Finn started as soon as the general contractor wanted, but she knew that it would take many days to complete the job. Drywall work was something that shouldn't be rushed!

Once the sheets of drywall were delivered, some of the MARSHALLTOWN tools—Hank Hammer, Nicki Knife, Rachel Rasp, Tina T-Square, Jill Jab Saw, Pete Panel Lifter—sprang into action, hanging the drywall to the wood studs.

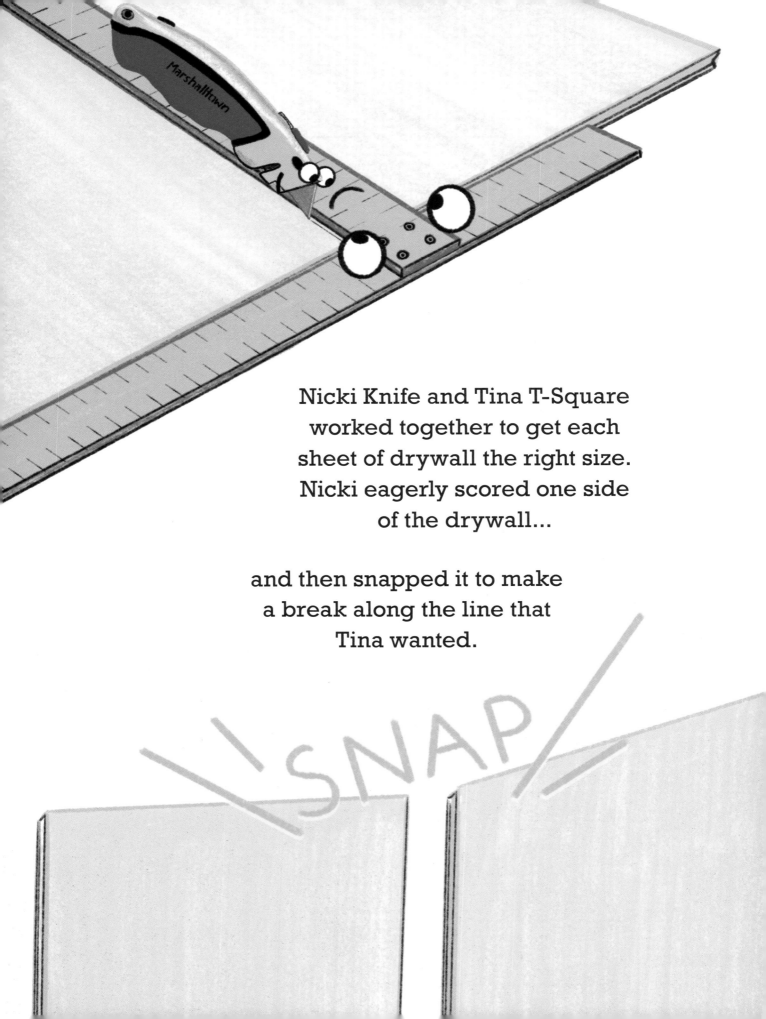

Nicki Knife and Tina T-Square
worked together to get each
sheet of drywall the right size.
Nicki eagerly scored one side
of the drywall...

and then snapped it to make
a break along the line that
Tina wanted.

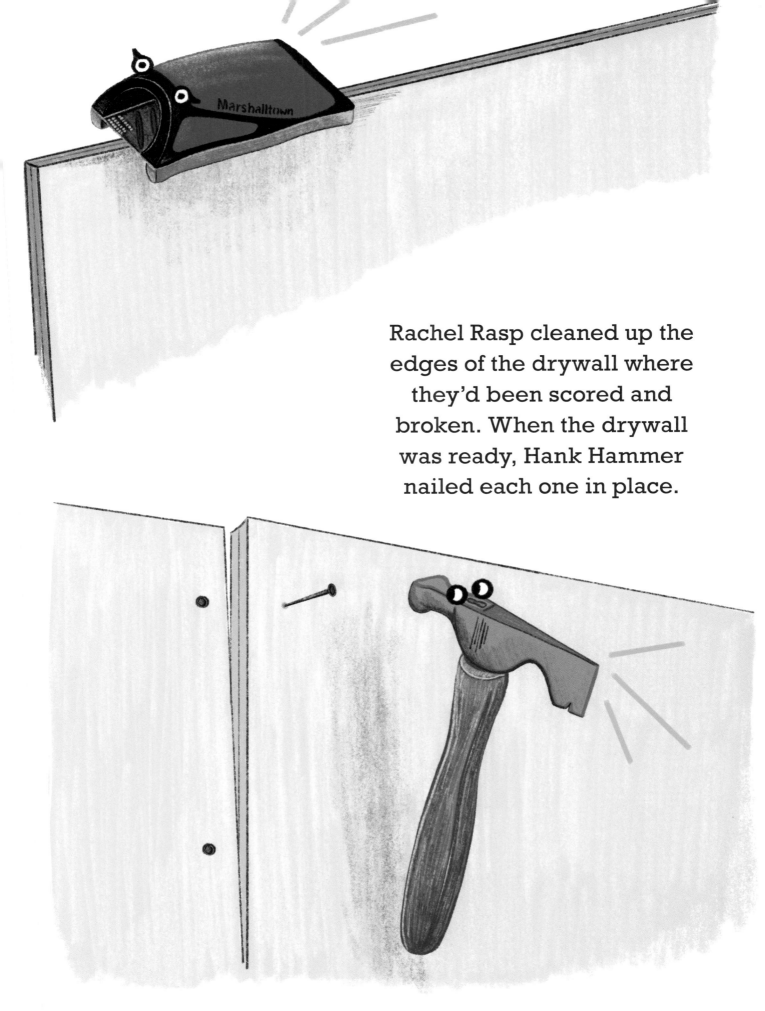

Rachel Rasp cleaned up the edges of the drywall where they'd been scored and broken. When the drywall was ready, Hank Hammer nailed each one in place.

Jill Jab Saw cut the rectangles in the drywall for electrical boxes

while Pete Panel Lifter lifted the sheets of drywall to the proper height.

Jill was weary from all the sawing, but she enjoyed looking at the work they had accomplished. Now that the drywall was hung, it was time for the finishing work to begin.

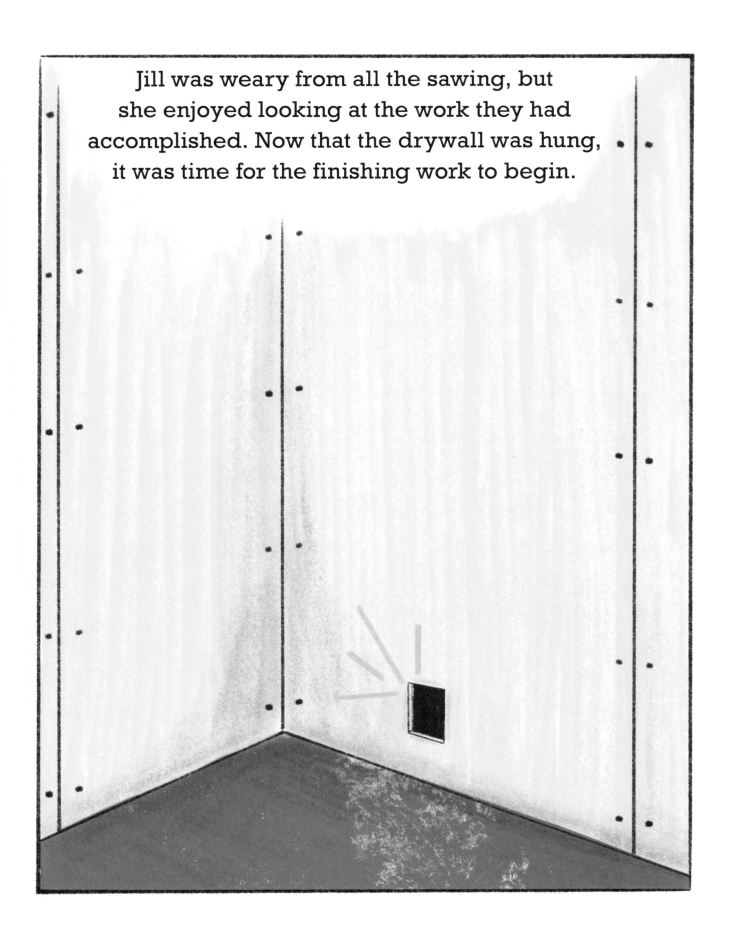

With Mary Mud Pan holding the joint compound, Johnny Joint Knife dove right into his work.

Johnny quickly spread the first coat of joint compound over all the tape, covering each and every joint where the sheets of drywall met. He made sure to cover every nail that Hank Hammer had used to hold the sheets to the studs.

After giving the first coat of joint compound time to dry, Mary Mud Pan and Johnny Joint Knife worked together again to cover the first coat with a bit more joint compound. Tammy Taping Knife came in and feathered the edges of the joint compound so that it blended nicely with the drywall.

The next day Mary Mud Pan
carried more joint compound while
Tammy Taping Knife effortlessly
spread a thin, final coat. Again,
she feathered the edges, making
everything smooth and flush.

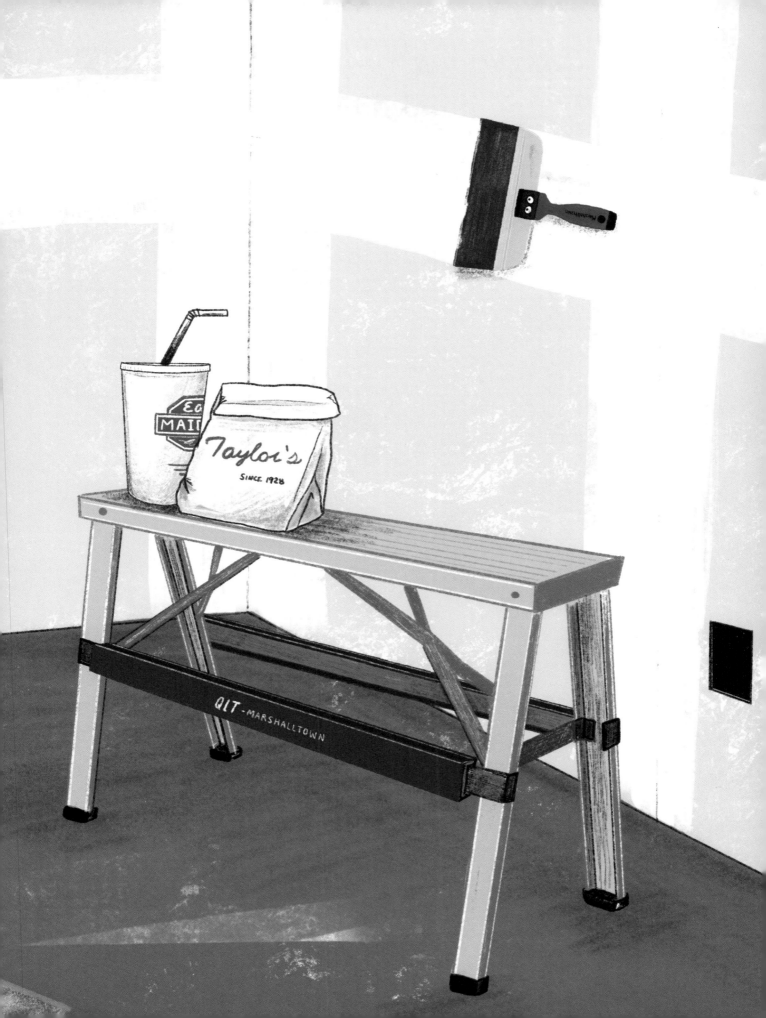

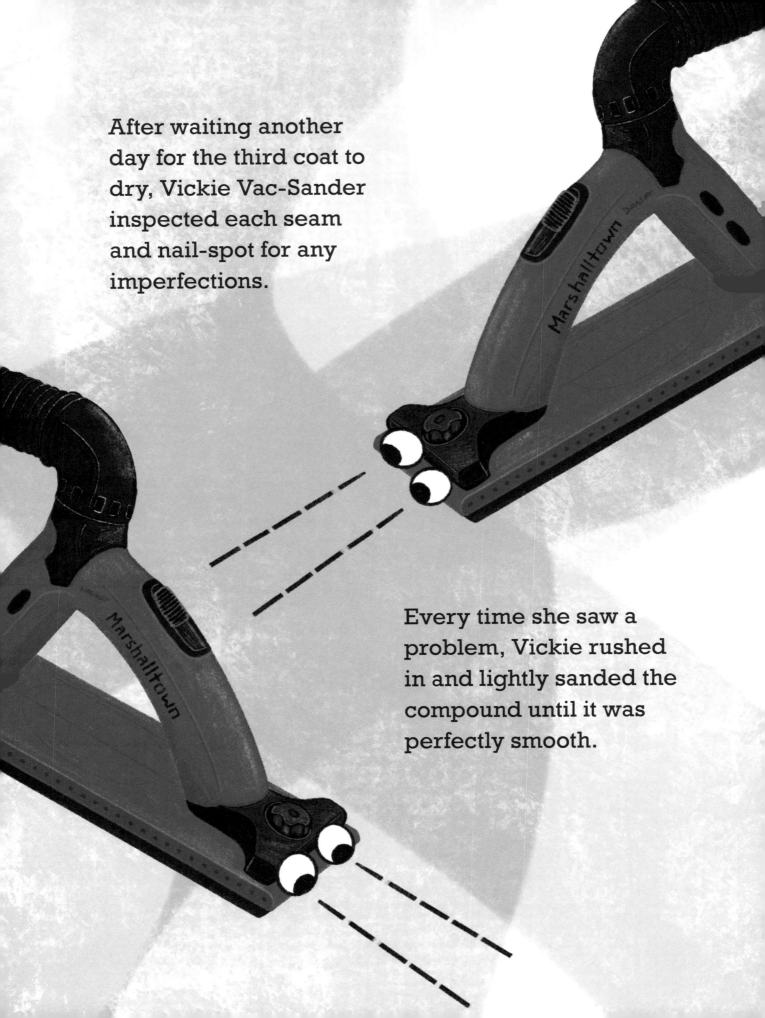

After waiting another day for the third coat to dry, Vickie Vac-Sander inspected each seam and nail-spot for any imperfections.

Every time she saw a problem, Vickie rushed in and lightly sanded the compound until it was perfectly smooth.

Mr. Mason wanted the walls of each room to
be textured, so Ms. Finn asked Tim Texture
Sprayer to do the work. Tim had been
texturing for many years and had a lot of
experience doing large projects. His large,
16-gallon tank would help to make
quick work of each room.

But Henry Hopper Gun, Tim's little brother, had hoped Ms. Finn would use him and his 2-gallon hopper on the job. Henry looked up to his brother and always wanted to do everything he did. A few tears started to come from his eyes when Henry realized that Tim would do all the work.

Marshall T. Trowel could see what was happening and he spoke softly to Henry.

"Henry, one day you'll be older like your big brother, Tim, but today he's bigger, more experienced and the right tool for this job. Ms. Finn is making her best choice, but she still loves you and appreciates the work that you do. I know you could do the work very well, but you'll get your chance another day."

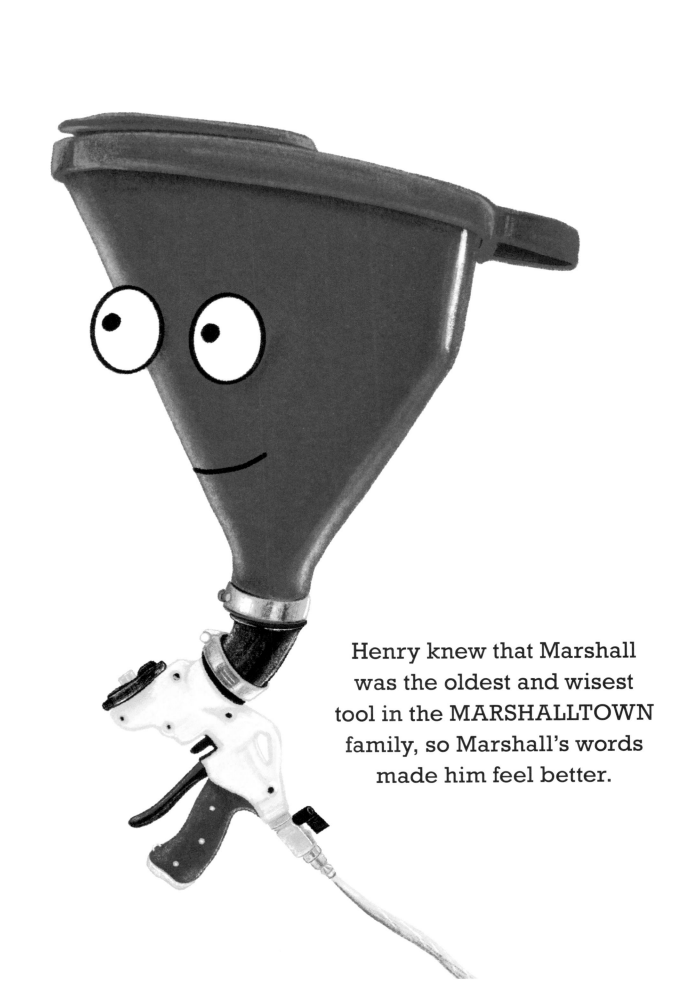

Henry knew that Marshall
was the oldest and wisest
tool in the MARSHALLTOWN
family, so Marshall's words
made him feel better.

"Ms. Finn spent many years perfecting her skills in the drywall trade. She wanted to run her own business and reached that goal by working hard.

You can be anything you want to be! If you practice and practice, you'll be able to reach your goals, too!

Try not to compare yourself to your big brother, or anyone else for that matter. It's important that you give your best effort to be the best you can be!"

Tim Texture Sprayer finished spraying texture on the walls of the house. Tim was proud of his work, but Henry was even prouder of his big brother.

Henry told Tim,
"You did a great job on all that texturing! I'm so proud of you and the great work you do. I'm going to keep working on my texturing skills so that I can be the best I can be."

JOE CARTER is the husband to his wonderful wife Janelle and the father to three fantastic children: Michael, Hanna and Samuel. Joe grew up in the small, northern Iowa community of Hanlontown. He graduated from North Central-Manly High School and later, Iowa State University with an Industrial Engineering degree. Joe worked as an engineer for General Motors and Rockwell International before he began a long career with MARSHALLTOWN, a U.S. manufacturer of high-quality construction tools.

Between times of working as an engineer, Joe graduated from law school at the University of Arkansas and practiced law with Strong and Associates in Springfield, Missouri. He returned to MARSHALLTOWN and moved to Marshalltown, Iowa. In 1998 Joe became the president of MARSHALLTOWN and later added CEO to that title.

Joe met the love of his life, Janelle Andersen, at Iowa State University where she also graduated with an Industrial Engineering degree. Janelle worked for General Motors, R.R. Donnelley & Sons, and MARSHALLTOWN. Today she works on the local school board, special business projects, and the Board of Directors for Farmers Savings Bank.

HANNA CARTER is an illustrator and graphic designer. She grew up in Marshalltown, Iowa and graduated from Iowa State University in Ames, Iowa. She moved to Oregon after college in 2016.

Hanna has loved both books and drawing for as long as she can remember. In fact, her first job was at the Marshalltown Public Library, where she spent a lot of her time leafing through children's books. She's pretty psyched that she got to make her own books with her dad.

Hanna has worked on editorial illustrations, book covers, animations, comics, children's books, brand merchandise, and exhibits her artwork in galleries. She makes illustrations and animations about food-related things for the *Los Angeles Times*, *VinePair*, and other publications.

Hanna lives in Portland, Oregon with her boyfriend, Chris and many, many books.

Other Marshall T. Trowel and Family books:

Marshall T. Trowel and Family - Concrete - Work Hard. Work Together.

Learn more at www.marshallttrowel.com